Text and illustrations copyright © Éditions Palette 2008
First published under the title *Alphab'art: les lettres cachées dans l'art*
by Éditions Palette, Paris, France

First published in Great Britain in 2009 and in the USA in 2010 by
Frances Lincoln Children's Books,
4 Torriano Mews, Torriano Avenue, London NW5 2RZ
www.franceslincoln.com

Text and picture selection by Anne Guéry and Olivier Dussutour
English translation © Antonia Parkin 2009
Design concept by Loïc Le Gall

British Library Cataloguing in Publication Data available on request

ISBN: 978-1-84780-013-8

Printed in Italy

9 8 7 6 5 4 3 2 1

Anne Guéry - Olivier Dussutour

Alphab'art

Find the letters hidden in the paintings

F
FRANCES LINCOLN
CHILDREN'S BOOKS

A

Find the letter A hiding

in this painting by

Giotto

Giotto, *The Life of Saint Francis*, 1297-1299

Find the letter B hiding in this painting by

B

Combas

Robert Combas, *Portrait Presumed to be Christian Boltanski*, 1987

Find the letter C hiding in this painting by

Chagall

Marc Chagall, *The Crow who Wanted to Imitate the Eagle*, 1947

D

Find the letter D hiding in this painting by

Picasso

Pablo Picasso, *Head*, 1913

Find the letter E

hiding in

this painting by

Salvador Dalí, *Giraffe on Fire*, 1936-1937

Find the letter F

hiding in

this painting by

Mondrian

Piet Mondrian (1872-1944), *Composition with Red, Blue and Yellow*, 1930, oil on canvas, 46 x 46 cm © 2008 Mondrian/Holtzman Trust c/o HCR International Virginia USA

Find the letter G hiding in this painting by

Miró

Joan Miró, *Figures and Birds Dancing against a Blue Sky with Stars*, 25 May 1968

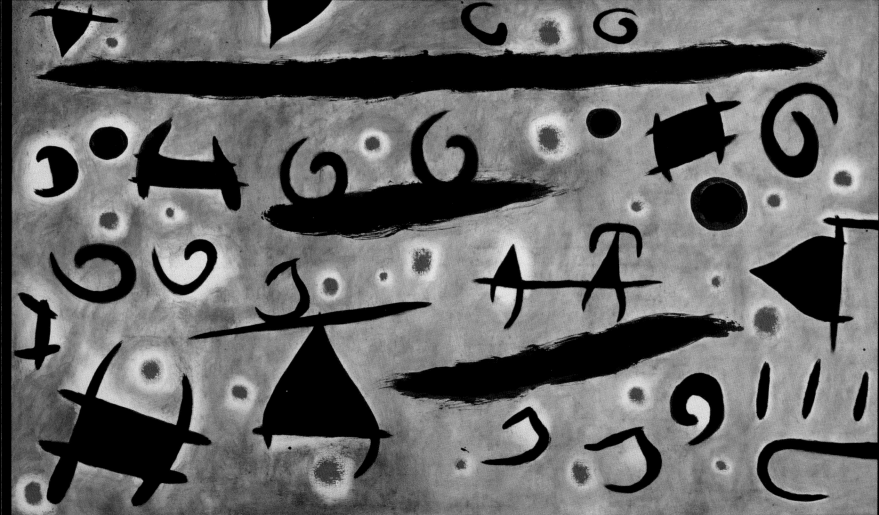

Find the letter H hiding in this painting by

Manet

Édouard Manet, *Races at Longchamp*, 1866

Find the letter i hiding in this painting by

Hopper

Edward Hopper, *Gas*, 1940

Find the letter J hiding in this painting by

Kandinsky

Vassily Kandinsky, *Red Oval*, 1920

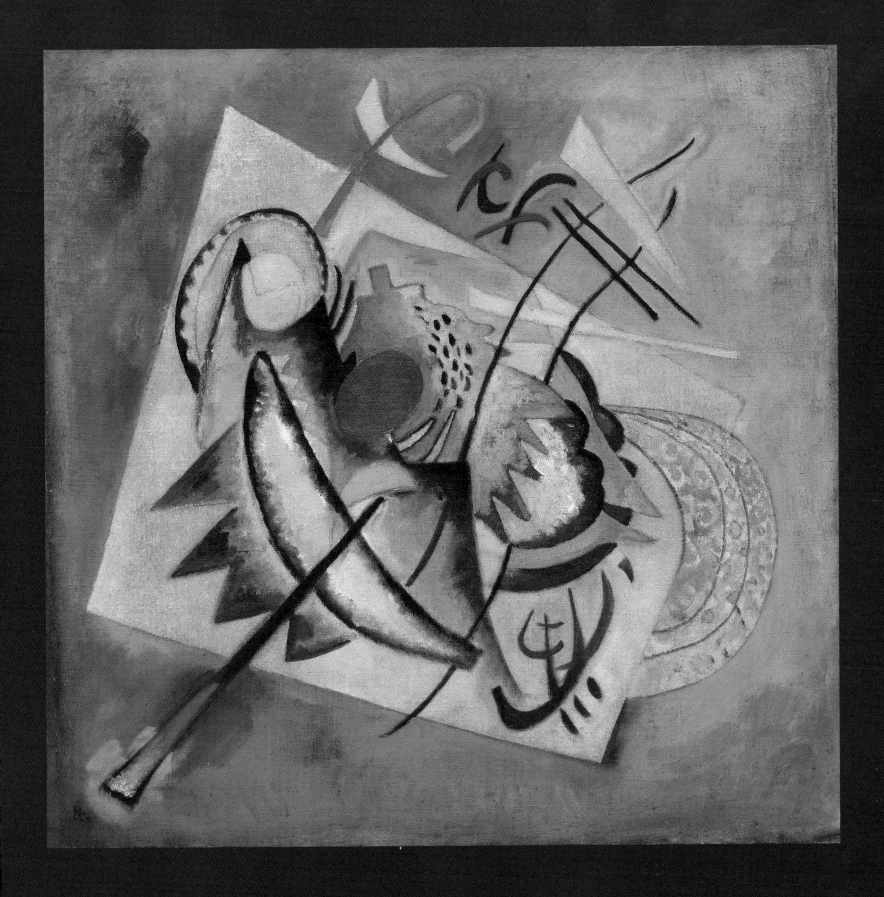

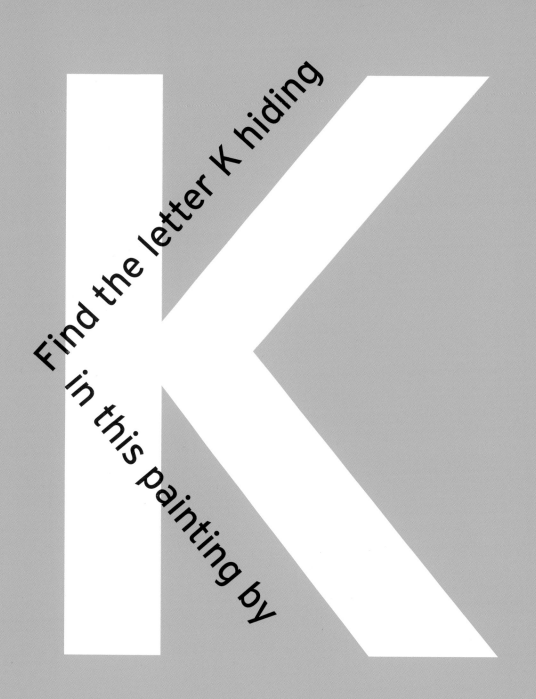

Find the letter K hiding in this painting by

Delaunay

Robert Delaunay, *Champ de Mars: Red Tower*, 1911

Find the letter L hiding in this painting by

Bosch

Hieronymus Bosch, *The Wayfarer* or *The Prodigal Son*, about 1510

Find the letter M hiding in this painting by

Della Francesca

Piero Della Francesca, *Madonna and Child*, 1472-1474

Find the letter N hiding in this painting by

Uccello

Paolo Uccello, *The Battle of San Romano*, about 1450

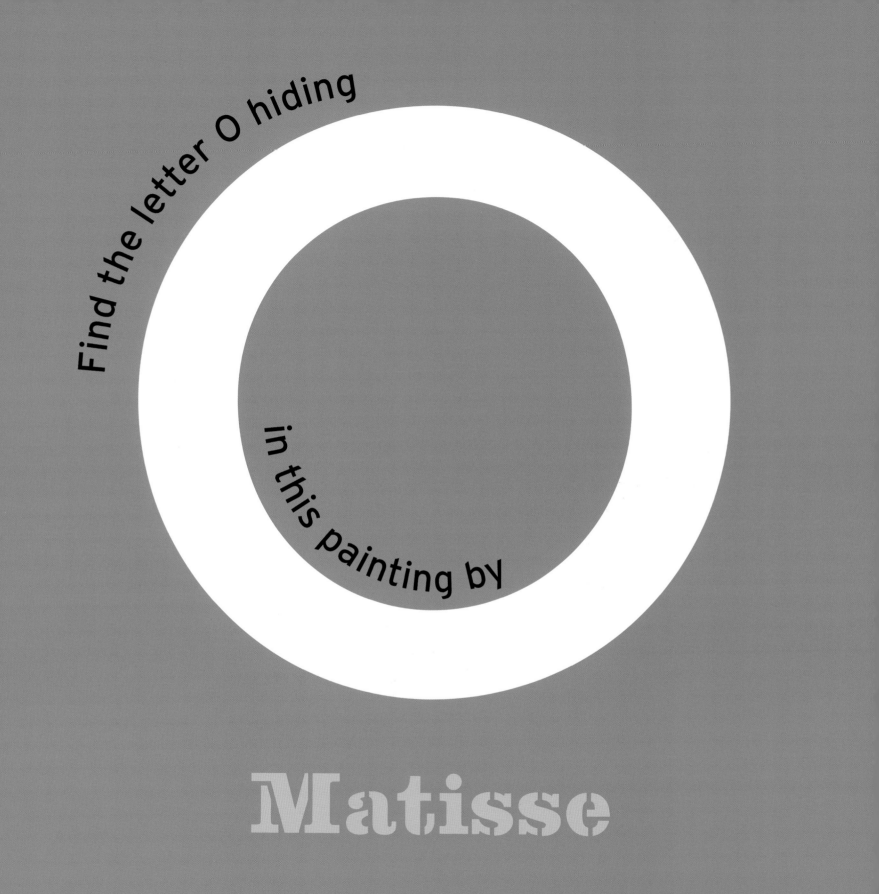

Find the letter O hiding in this painting by

Matisse

Henri Matisse, *The Inhabited Silence of Houses*, 1952

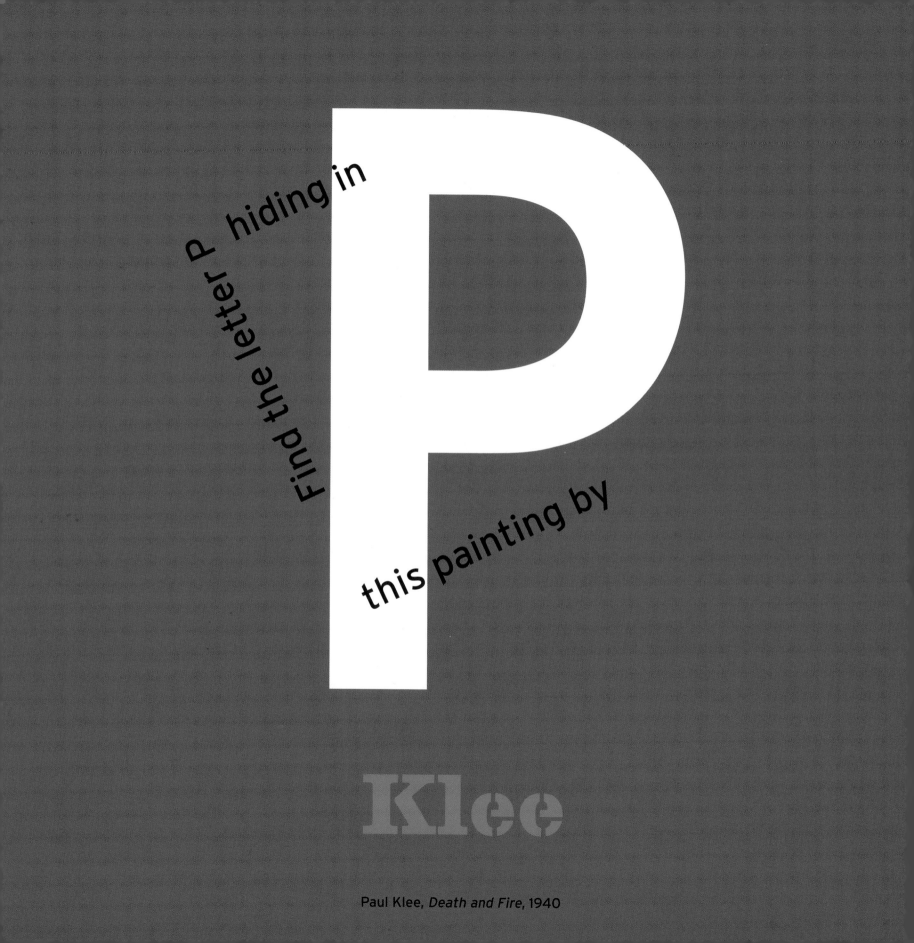

Find the letter P hiding in this painting by

P

Klee

Paul Klee, *Death and Fire*, 1940

Find the letter Q hiding in this painting by

Arcimboldo

Giuseppe Arcimboldo, *Fire*, 1566

R

Find the   letter R hiding

in this painting by

Magritte

René Magritte, *The Art of Conversation*, 1950

Find the letter S hiding in this painting by

Malevitch

Kazimir Malevitch, *Composition with Mona Lisa, Partial Eclipse*, 1914

T

Find the letter T hiding in this painting by

Vuillard

Édouard Vuillard, *In Bed*, 1891

Find the letter U hiding in this painting by

Dubuffet

Jean Dubuffet, *Cloth of Episodes*, 1976

Find the letter V hiding

in this painting by

Van Gogh

Vincent Van Gogh, *Portrait of Armand Roulin*, 1888

Find the letter W hiding in this painting by

La Tour

Georges de La Tour, *The Adoration of the Shepherds*, about 1644

Find the letter X hiding in this painting by

Raoul Dufy, *14th July, 1907*

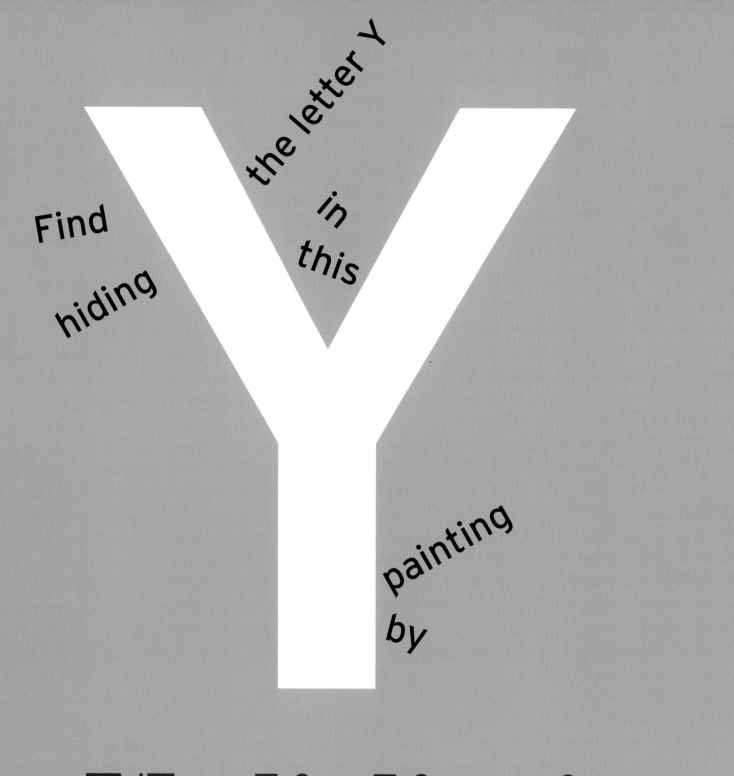

Find hiding the letter Y in this painting by

Modigliani

Amedeo Modigliani, *Tree and Houses*, 1919

Find the letter Z hiding in this painting by

Picabia

Francis Picabia, *The Cacodylic Eye*, 1921

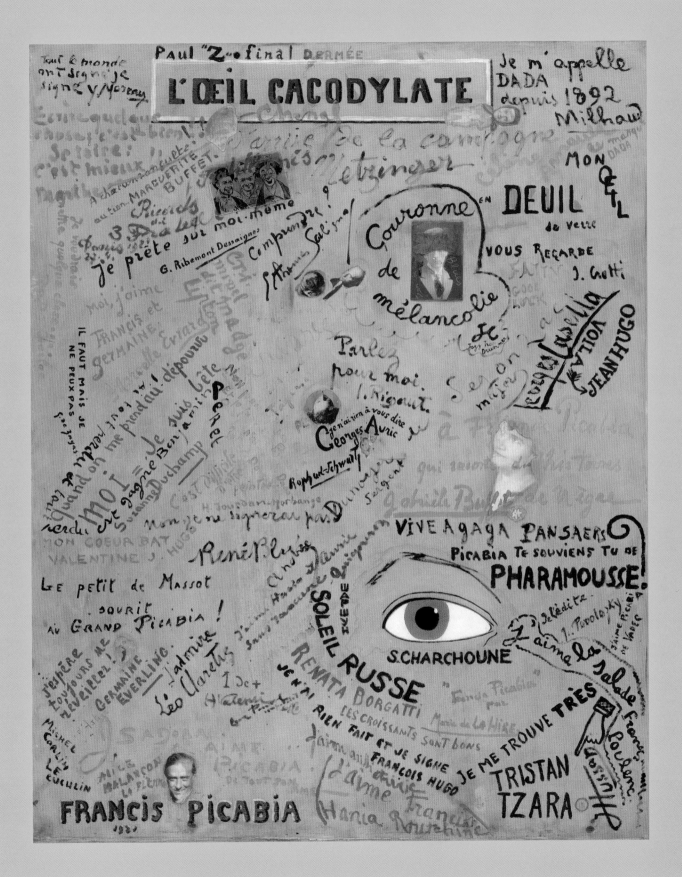

A 13TH CENTURY
The Life of Saint Francis, 1297-1299
> GIOTTO di Bondone (1266-1337), Italian painter, sculptor and architect

At the heart of the Middle Ages, the artist Giotto achieved an illusion of depth in his architectural paintings that had never been seen before. In this fresco it is almost as if Giotto is creating a piece of scenery for the stage or painting three-dimensional houses inside which real people are cowering, hiding from the enormous demons flying above the city.

B 20TH CENTURY
Portrait presumed to be Christian Boltanski, 1987
> Robert COMBAS (born 1957), French painter

Two strange skeletons dance around this portrait of Christian Boltanski, Combas's friend and fellow artist. Combas likes to make links between classical references and popular culture: here he depicts a traditional dance of death using a light-hearted comic-book style. Combas is the founder of the French artistic movement known as Free Figuration (*Figuration Libre*).

C 20TH CENTURY
The Crow who Wanted to Imitate the Eagle, 1947
> Marc CHAGALL (1887-1985), French painter of Russian origin

A crow, trying to compete with his rival the eagle, attempts to carry off a sheep in his talons. Chagall brings to life this fable by La Fontaine using bold but delicate brushstrokes on a canvas that is reminiscent of the colourful paintings of his Russian Jewish heritage.

D 20TH CENTURY
Head, 1913
> Pablo PICASSO (1881-1973), Spanish painter and sculptor

What a strange head! Is this a man or a woman? Which way is it facing? In this work Picasso is deliberately breaking down the shapes we see in everyday life: nothing is recognisable any longer. Even the idea of painting itself has been cast aside – this image is made up of paper collage. Picasso was the founder of the Cubist movement and one of the greatest artists of the 20th Century.

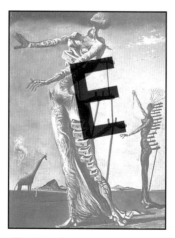

E 20TH CENTURY
Giraffe on Fire, 1936-1937
> Salvador DALÍ (1904 -1989), Spanish painter

A giraffe in flames and human figures with drawers emerging from their bodies? What a weird landscape this is. Dali likes to tell strange stories and depict disconcerting scenes in his paintings. He drew images from his imagination and his subconscious, and was inspired by the random association of shapes and objects. This style of painting is known as Surrealism.

F 20TH CENTURY
Composition with Red, Blue and Yellow, 1930
> Piet MONDRIAN (1872-1944), Dutch painter

Mondrian applies his own theories to this painting, paring it down to a composition of the three primary colours arranged on a framework of black horizontal and vertical lines. Mondrian (along with Kandinsky and Malevitch) is one of the major figures in abstract art. He removed every superfluous line, colour and image from his paintings in his attempt to devise a universal pictorial language.

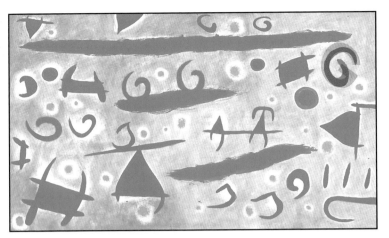

G **20TH CENTURY**
Figures and Birds Dancing against a Blue Sky with Stars, 25 May 1968
> Joan MIRÓ (1893–1983), Spanish painter and sculptor

In a similar way to the Surrealists, Miró leads us into a fantastical universe populated by strange beings, tiny unidentifiable creatures, floating shapes and graphic images. Drawn directly from Miró's imagination, these symbols seem to hover and move around one another against a highly coloured dream-like background. Miró's favourite themes in his paintings are women, birds and stars.

H **19TH CENTURY**
Races at Longchamp, 1866
> Édouard MANET (1832–1883), French painter

This painting represents another astonishing breakthrough in artistic tradition. Up until now almost all paintings have taken a religious or historical subject, but here we see a scene from everyday life: a race course with galloping horses throwing up clouds of dust with their hooves. Manet's paintings were seen as shocking, even scandalous, by the French art critics of his time, not simply because of his subjects, but also because of the free style he used to portray them. Here he wants to reproduce the blurry effect of bright light using rapidly applied touches of paint, which give the impression that the painting isn't even finished. This style led the way to what we think of as modern painting.

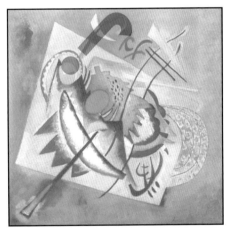

I **20TH CENTURY**
Gas, 1940
> Edward HOPPER (1882–1967), American painter

At first glance this painting seems almost like a photograph of an ordinary petrol station. Looking closer, though, we see the tiny figure of a man alone in the vast landscape and notice the impersonal feeling, the cold light and the disquieting but intriguing sense of emptiness that characterise the very particular style of this American painter of everyday life.

J **20TH CENTURY**
Red Oval, 1920
> Vassily KANDINSKY (1866–1944), Russian painter

No identifiable objects appear in this piece by Kandinsky. He developed a whole theory and language for abstract art, using graphic images and colours that fill and spill over the boundaries of the shapes he created. Kandinsky was attempting to draw the things he could not see: his hidden, spiritual intimations. For him, form and line are as expressive as a musical score.

K **20TH CENTURY**
Champ de Mars: Red Tower, 1911
> Robert DELAUNAY (1885–1941), French painter

This bright red Eiffel Tower seems to breathe and vibrate as though it were alive! The scene is almost ready to explode and fragment into a kaleidoscopic image. Colours play an enormously important role in the paintings of Delaunay, who was another pioneer of abstract art.

L 16TH CENTURY
The Wayfarer or *The Prodigal Son*, about 1510
> Jérôme BOSCH (1453-1516), Dutch painter

Bosch is the painter of monsters and all the creatures of the Underworld. He illustrated many biblical scenes, often including depictions of heaven and hell. Instead of trying to get closer to a representation of reality, Bosch preferred to evoke a fantastical world. Here the emphasis is on the feelings of the characters in the scene: the strange and uncomfortable traveller, the people hiding in and around the house, and the animals lifted straight out of a fairy tale.

M 15TH CENTURY
Madonna and Child, 1472-1474
> Piero Della FRANCESCA (1416-1492), Italian painter

Piero Della Francesca is one of the most important painters of the mid-15th century (the Italian Quattrocento). His treatment of light in this painting is a real innovation, and the figures illuminated by the soft glow he has perfected seem perfectly calm. In this religious scene the Virgin Mary and Jesus are held within an alcove, the geometric perspective of the domed ceiling reinforcing the meditative stance of the figures.

N 15TH CENTURY
The Battle of San Romano, about 1450
> Paolo UCCELLO (1397-1475), Italian painter

In this battle scene the sense of space is defined and delineated by the banner and lances in the foreground and by the fields in the background. Fascinated by perspective, Uccello divided up his canvases almost like geometrical jigsaws. The resulting paintings sometimes seem rather rigid and artificial, with figures who look more like toy soldiers than real people. Uccello was a fresco painter and is considered to be one of the fathers of the Italian Renaissance.

O 20TH CENTURY
The Inhabited Silence of Houses, 1952
> Henri MATISSE (1869-1954), French painter and sculptor

Both figures here are reduced to very basic shapes with plain ovals for their heads. This scene communicates a certain peaceful joy and Matisse has used only four colours (blue, yellow, black and white) and a simplified composition to define the three distinct areas of the canvas: the wall, the people at the table and the exterior scene. Matisse uses colour to sculpt shapes and to allow a drawing to take on form.

P 20TH CENTURY
Death and Fire, 1940
> Paul KLEE (1879-1940), Swiss painter

Paul Klee's art is all about making the invisible visible. Here Death is represented by simple graphic shapes on a background of intense, flat colour. Klee plays with signs he himself has invented, as though he is composing a musical score. He depicts a dreamlike, poetic world between those of Surrealism and Abstraction, and plays a very important role in the evolution of 20th Century art.

Q 16TH CENTURY
Fire, 1566
> Giuseppe ARCIMBOLDO (1527-1593), Italian painter

Another strange portrait! Here Arcimboldo constructs a face using objects that are all associated with fire: flames for the hair, flint irons for the nose and ears, and a candle for the neck. Arcimboldo was a painter-magician with an extraordinary imagination. He also painted portraits representing the four seasons using images of fruit, flowers and even vegetables. All these paintings are allegories that evoke the power of the Austrian Emperor for whom he worked.

R 20TH CENTURY
The Art of Conversation, 1950
> René MAGRITTE (1898–1967), Belgian painter

Huge stones are piled on top of one another to reveal the French word "RÊVE", which means 'dream'. This desert landscape might seem real but Magritte plays with the familiar elements of his painting to create a fantastical scene. He distorts scale and separates words from their meanings. This light-hearted work has been developed from Magritte's questioning of everything that we see and understand, which resulted in ordinary things suddenly becoming strange and poetical.

S 20TH CENTURY
Composition with Mona Lisa, Partial Eclipse, 1914
> Kazimir MALEVITCH (1878–1935), Russian painter

What is going on here? Are we in a Russian café, leafing through a newspaper? Or is this just a pile of cut up pictures? He uses several different media at once: paper collage, paint and writing in order to provoke new sensations in the onlooker. He is considered one of the masters of abstract art thanks to his inventive usage of simple geometrical shapes.

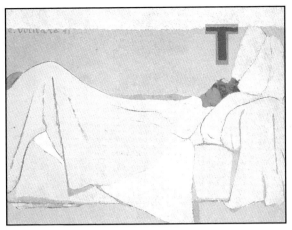

T 19TH CENTURY
In Bed, 1891
> Édouard VUILLARD (1868–1940), French painter

The sleeping figure in this painting seems lost amongst the materials of the bedroom. The colours, all different shades of grey, create a series of flat surfaces without perspective, broken up with lines made by heavy brushstrokes. Vuillard painted real subjects, often depicting domestic interiors, but wasn't constrained by the traditional rules of painting. His ornamental style depended as much on his memories as on observation.

U 20TH CENTURY
Cloth of Episodes, 1976
> Jean DUBUFFET (1901–1985), French painter and sculptor

Simplified figures are swamped by their surroundings made up of abstract scribbles and graffiti. And if this painting seems as though it could be the work of a child, this is because Dubuffet considered art to belong to everyone, not just the specialists. He used everyday found objects to create a new imaginary space. Outsider Art (*L'Art Brut*) is born.

V 19TH CENTURY
Portrait of Armand Roulin, 1888
> Vincent Van GOGH (1853–1890), Dutch painter

Van Gogh, like the other Impressionists, would often paint outdoors, and sought not to reproduce what he saw but to paint what he felt. Here, with broad, swift brushstrokes he creates a portrait of a man with a somewhat melancholy expression. The colours he uses are striking: the shadows are not black, but loaded with blue paint; the pure yellow of the man's jacket captures and reflects the light.

W 17TH CENTURY
The Adoration of the Shepherds, about 1644
> Georges de LA TOUR (1593–1652), French painter

In this night-time scene the absence of decoration and the circle formed by the figures invite us to join the intimate group. Using a chiaroscuro (light and shade) technique, de La Tour contrasts the areas of shadow and bright light on the canvas. The faint glimmer given off by the candle is not sufficient to explain the luminence reflected in the faces of Mary, Joseph and the shepherds. So where is the light coming from?

X 20TH CENTURY
14th July, 1907
> Raoul DUFY (1877–1953), French painter

This scene depicting the 14th July Bastille Day celebrations is imbued with a joyful and festive atmosphere. Dufy's painting style is innovative – his shapes are much simplified, and the colours are pure, as though he is using paint straight out of the tubes. Dufy painted very quickly, trying to capture the immediacy of the present moment. His brushstrokes are broad and rapid and you can still see the canvas between and underneath the areas of paint. This audacity characterised the Fauvist movement of which Dufy was part.

Y 20TH CENTURY
Tree and Houses, 1919
> Amedeo MODIGLIANI (1884–1920), Italian painter

Modigliani has framed this strange painting as though it were the portrait of a person. He treats the tree like an elongated face with hollow eyes and a melancholy stance. Modigliani liked to depict real scenes, and, like a sculptor, creates solid shapes with his paintbrush. Line is more important than texture in this painting in which the sombre colours are applied thinly over the canvas.

Z 20TH CENTURY
The Cacodylic Eye, 1921
> Francis PICABIA (1879–1953), French painter

"I love salad" "My heart is beating" "I have done nothing and yet I sign"...
Picabia asked his friends to join him in the creation of this painting by writing these ironic statements on the canvas. Picabia was working within a new artistic movement known as Dada (a word chosen at random from the dictionary, and which means hobby-horse). The provocative attitude of the Dada artists was indicative of their desire to express themselves freely without any restraints whatsoever.